The Face of Victory

Tom Tirivangani

Published by
Tom Tirivangani Press and Publications
200 Sanford Ave North, Hamilton, Ontario
Canada L8L5Z8

Copyright © 2025 by Tom Tirivangani
All rights reserved. All rights reserved.
No part of this publication may be reproduced, stored in a retrieval system, or transmitted in any form or by any means except in the case of a brief quotation printed in articles or reviews without prior permission in writing from the publisher

First Printing, 2025

Unless otherwise identified, Scripture quotations are taken from the New King James Version®. Copyright © 1982 by Thomas Nelson. Used by permission. All rights reserved.

Scripture quotations identified NIV are taken from the NEW INTERNATIONAL VERSION, Holy Bible, New International Version®, NIV® Copyright ©1973, 1978, 1984, 2011 by Biblica, Inc.® Used by permission. All rights reserved worldwide.

Scripture quotations identified AMPC are taken from the Amplified Bible, Classic Edition. Copyright © 1954, 1958, 1962, 1964, 1965, 1987 by The Lockman Foundation

Contents

Preface	1
1 Our Road Map For the Futute	2
2 The Man Behind the Vision	7
3 The Vision	12
4 Understanding the Vision of the Church	21
5 Essential Aspects of the Vision	24
6 Our Mission	28
7 The Pattern for the Church	29
8 Whose Church is it?	34
9 A Word on Being One Body	38
10 A Word on Church Membership	41
11 Leadership Structure	46
12 The Blessing of Serving in Another Man's Ministry	47

Preface

This revised edition of the Church Vision Book was written under divine inspiration, as I was led by God to make the vision clear on tablets, so that anyone who reads it may run with it. I embarked on a journey to revise the Vision Book and, in this edition, have also included the Church Constitution. The Constitution reflects our statement of faith and outlines the guidelines for church governance.

1

Our Road Map For the Futute

Without a vision, people perish, and without faith, a vision is dead. Every journey of faith begins with a single step. Every great cathedral standing today started with the laying of one single brick. Everything God does starts small; it is always the story of a mustard seed.

The seed begins as the smallest of all seeds, but it grows into a large tree that provides comfort and refuge for the birds of the air (Matt. 13.31–32). Although the seed is small, faith causes it to grow into something great and significant (Matt. 17.20). This is the mystery that reveals the power in the Word of God.

The Word of God contains potent power that is unleashed through faith and by acting on the Word. Real faith, born out of our affinity with the Word of God, carries the miracle seed for change and transformation. The change we desire to see in the world is a product of our faith.

The story of how Christ's Voice of Restoration Ministries began is a mystery; it is the mystery of what faith can do. The church that started with a family of four is growing into a multinational and multiracial church impacting nations. This is a reflection of the inexpressible mystery of the power of the Cross of our Lord Jesus Christ.

Christ died to give you a place in His Kingdom. As Scripture testifies: "The Spirit Himself bears witness with our spirit that we are children of God, and if children, then heirs—heirs of God and joint heirs with Christ" (Rom. 8.16–17).

This book you are holding in your hand is a powerful tool to help you understand the vision of the church and the guidelines you are expected to observe as you take your place in the Kingdom of God and move the vision of the church forward.

Our lives are to be lived with purpose and principle. That is how Christ lived His life, and we are called to imitate Him. As a believer and a member of both the Kingdom of God and the Church of God, you must come to the understanding that Jesus Christ died to give you this place in the Kingdom. He paid the price to qualify you for it, He paid with His own blood.

The vision you are about to read did not just come from the imagination of a man. It is Christ who birthed both the vision and the church through His death on the Cross, and He gave this vision to His servant, Prophet Tom Tirivangani. This is the revelation of Jesus Christ, which God gave Him (Christ) to show to his servant, Prophet Tom Tirivangani, what he must do to prepare for the coming back of our Lord Jesus Christ.

This vision was made known by Jesus Christ, who died but now lives forever, when He revealed it to His servant, the prophet of God. Christ did this by sending his angel to the prophet, Tom Tirivangani.

Blessed are those who read the words of the vision and obey it. Blessed also are those who hear the words of the vision by the help of the Holy Spirit and take to heart what is written in this book, making every effort to do the work of God. It is this very work of God in which we are engaged in that will usher in the second coming of our Lord Jesus Christ (Rev.1.1-3)

The Coming of Christ is the true hope the world is waiting for, everything else is a waste of time. Glory be to God in the highest!

This vision is a holy revelation from Christ, given to the man of God to inspire the people of God to return to God and take their rightful positions in the Kingdom of God, as we wait for the coming of the Bridegroom.

By reading this book, you will understand how this ministry started and what is on the mind of God concerning the Church and His work. The Church did not just start; it was a divine commission from above. Scripture testifies that whatever is from above is above all things. Whatever is born of God overcomes the world, and this is the source of our victory, our faith in the risen Christ: "Now this is the confidence that we have in Him, that if we ask anything according to His will, He hears us" (1 John 5:14).

The book will also explain to you the secret behind the Cross of Calvary. It offers heavenly insight into the very cause of the death and resurrection of Jesus Christ. As you participate actively and faithfully in the vision of the Church of God, your life will never be the same again.

You are part of an end-time, non-denominational, prophetic ministry and Church of God. This is a model church for Christ, a model of how He wants His Bride to be before His second coming. It is a Church that must be without wrinkle, blemish, or any such thing.

The church began as an ordinary mustard seed and has continued to grow. But remember, anything that looks like and belongs to Jesus Christ will face opposition and persecution from the enemy. Though the Church may have gone through challenges, we are assured of victory:

> For they intended evil against You; they devised a plot which they are not able to perform. (Ps. 21.11)
>
> They will fight against you, but they shall not prevail against you. For I am with you," says the Lord, "to deliver you. (Jer. 1.19)

The Church may seem small now, but the vision is very big. Here, we stand on the mountain top of faith. You are called to demonstrate your faith by waiting for the vision to manifest. Be patient. A time is coming when everything will be big and in its rightful place, for the glory of God. What may have appeared to be a small church will become a church that reaches across nations and generations.

The Church you are part of is not just an ordinary church; it is the revelation of Jesus Christ for the end times. This is a vision unlike any other.

> And so it was, when Jesus had ended these sayings, that the people were astonished at His teaching, for He taught them as one having authority, and not as the scribes. (Matt. 7.28-29)

Prophet Tom Tirivangani, like his Master Jesus Christ, is a unique and different man of God. He is unlike any other. He has been specially prepared for this end-time dispensation and harvest. He is marked by a deep longing and a rare passion to see the full manifestation of Christ in His Church. The Church must give Christ His rightful place, as the Chief Shepherd, the Chief Cornerstone, and the Rock upon which the Church is built.

Prophet Tom Tirivangani declares:

> "I know what the Lord wants to do in this Church. The Lord has given me His blueprint, His pattern for the Church, which I now share with you. I urge you and implore you: join hands with me to fulfill the vision of Christ."

Can you be the man or woman who will stand as a pillar in the Church of God? Can you accept your call and make a difference in our generation? Christ is calling you. Will you deny Him? Will you be ashamed of Him? Will you make excuses in the face of His great sacrifice? What will you give Him for all He has done for you (Ps.116.12).

Make up your mind. Be part of a dynamic revelation and vision that is inspired and led by the Spirit of God. This is a vision destined to change nations, and to change the world.

2

The Man Behind the Vision

Prophet Tom Tirivangani was born in Zimbabwe. The grace of God has always been a major factor in his life. Even at a time when Tom did not walk right with God, God continued to walk faithfully with him. The hand of God was upon him from the beginning.

In early June of 1974, when Tom was still a young boy, his uncle Peter would often call him in their local dialect, "Thomas Mudzidzi WaJesu," which literally translates to "Thomas, the disciple of Jesus Christ." Even then, Prophet Tom Tirivangani bore the marks of discipleship to Jesus Christ.

He was raised by strict, charismatic Catholic parents who instilled in him the virtues of discipline, hard work, and love for others. Their deep care and generosity had a profound impact on Tom's life. The family home became a place of refuge for many in the community, especially the poor. His mother was always giving, if it wasn't salt, it was cornmeal; one day it might be clothes, another day money, or an offer of work.

Prophet Tom Tirivangani vividly recalls the years from 1976 to 1979, during the height of the war for independence in Zimbabwe. His father's three-bedroom house in the Western Triangle Suburbs of Highfield, Harare, housed six families during that time. How six families were able to share a 3-bedroom house for 3 years is the mystery of what love and faith can do. He never once heard his father or mother complain. They ate together, slept together, played together and lived together in unity. Little did young Tom know that God had already enrolled him in His own college, right there in his parents' home.

We as men have our own colleges, but a true man of God must enter the University of Jesus Christ, where the Holy Spirit is the perfect schoolmaster. Every challenge in life is a test that must be taken if one is to qualify as a man of God.

However, Tom used to struggle with his dark past. Satan knows those whom the Lord has prepared for Himself. His agenda is to eliminate them before they discover what God has called them to be. At the age of five, little Tom almost died after being struck with measles; an attack of the enemy. At sixteen, he survived an attempted murder on his life by one of Satan's messengers. Tom refused to press charges against the perpetrator, insisting on forgiveness. He surprised the police officer when he said that this act of evil must be left for God to judge. This has become a consistent pattern in his life: never to hold a grudge. The Man of God once said:

> "Whatever people say about me cannot change who I am. I am what God says I am. None of us can ever outgrow our need for forgiveness and our need to forgive. I need to forgive as I seriously need to be forgiven. Remember this; of him that hopes to be forgiven, it is required that he forgive. I owe everything to the grace of God."

The grace of God guided Prophet Tom Tirivangani out of his troubles. The grace of God was also upon him during his academic life. Popularly known as "Professor bookworm," Tom was a highly respected student at Howard Institute for his academic prowess. This reputation continued even into law school. He graduated at the top of his class at the University of Zimbabwe and received the Book

Prize for Academic Excellence. He was later awarded the Commonwealth Chevening Human Rights Scholarship in recognition of his extensive work in the field of human rights. He pursued a Master of Laws (LLM) degree at the University of Warwick and was awarded a British National Health Services bursary to study for a PhD at the University of Greenwich in the United Kingdom.

But today, all of that counts for nothing to him compared to the salvation he received. He proclaims: "That I am saved is the greatest thing. To me, the greatest thing has already happened, it is my salvation. Nothing I will ever do will surpass that."

However, at the height of his career, Tom drifted away from the Lord. He recalls:

> "I was in a dark pit of sin. I was the chief of all sinners. I saw no way out. I recognized that I could not help myself. I needed God. I cried out in my distress to the Lord, and He heard me.
>
> Miraculously, God visited me one night. I had an encounter with my Savior. There was no human preacher, but God Himself. That night, the chains were broken, and I was free. My life has never been the same again. Grace found me when sin had bound me in a prison. The real victory of faith is to trust God in the dark. Today, I am a servant of God; on God's part, an act of His grace; on my part, an act of gratitude to God. 'What shall I render to the Lord for all His benefits toward me?' (Ps. 116.12)"

"Called, tried, set apart, and chosen by grace and grace alone," according to Acts 13.2, is how Prophet Tom Tirivangani describes his calling and vocation as a servant of God. Truly, this is a vision unlike any other.

A man cannot serve God while he is still attached to the world. The servant of God must deny himself and forsake all to follow Christ. Prophet Tom Tirivangani left behind his career and business as a lawyer to follow Jesus Christ. It was by no means an easy decision, but one made in tears. He still feeds on those tears today.

It is true that many follow Jesus into the breaking of bread, but few are willing to drink from the cup of His passion. Many desire to rejoice with Jesus, but few are willing to endure anything for Him or with Him. Those who truly want to walk with Christ must prepare for a life of loneliness, few friends, persecutions, and trials. But for those who endure, the reward is eternal life.

Prophet Tom has endured name-calling, persecution, and hostility in the city of Hamilton, surprisingly, from many of those he prays for the most. When asked why he still prays fervently for those who revile and persecute him, his answer is this:

> "A true man of God's response must never be based on fluctuating emotions but on the Word of God. Christ, who said 'pray for your enemies,' was Himself humiliated by His enemies. We must never be controlled by what we hear or what we see. To do so is to fall into the schemes of the devil. Those who know God will never put their trust in man but in Jesus Christ. However, it is important to acknowledge that those who know the grace of God will never ignore man, because by His divine grace, God can turn an enemy into a friend, a prostitute into a woman of God as was the case with Mary Magdalene, and a persecutor like Saul of Tarsus into a great and mighty man of God, the Apostle Paul. Remember, God's grace can turn yesterday's enemies into tomorrow's allies."

Prophet Tom Further says, "Instead of revenge, I choose the path of love." It is therefore clear that no amount of rejection or hostility releases the Christian from the responsibility to act in a loving fashion. Come to our church and experience the true Love of God.

WHAT TO EXPECT

We believe that the Church is the highest institution in any nation in the world, and that it must be run and administered at the highest level of excellence. The Church is the only institution that relies absolutely on the Holy Spirit and the Word of God to conduct its affairs. It is, therefore, a mirror and reflection of true governance.

Every true church must have at the center of its core values a spirit of excellence in the manner in which it conducts its affairs. The Church mirrors the Spirit of Christ and His ethics and is a model of good governance. Its members and leaders must therefore commit themselves to the highest level of ethical conduct by observing the standard of Christ as given in the Word of God. "Let all things be done decently and in order" (1 Cor. 14.40).

In order to do this, and by inspiration of the Holy Spirit, Prophet Tom has devoted himself and the Church to build guidelines, systems, and structures that will help the Church achieve this goal. Every leader of the Church is expected to commit and devote himself or herself to upholding these guidelines, systems, and structures as a way of honoring Christ, who died and paid the price for the Church.

Serving Christ has always been a sacrifice. A man cannot serve Christ while he is still full of himself or herself. Serving Christ is a call to completely empty oneself, surrender one's life, and embrace the Spirit of Christ. This is necessary if one is to serve Him and bear fruit. Good leadership produces good fruit.

In response to God's call, the Man of God says, **"WE ARE UNSTOPPABLE."**

3

The Vision

"A man of vision and purpose sees opportunities in challenges" — Prophet Tom Tirivangani

Vision is the focus or target that gives life direction, purpose, and meaning. Vision is like the heart in the human body. Without it, there is no life. It is impossible to sustain life in any institution or organization without a vision.

Every genuine calling begins with a vision or dream, and that dream or vision must come from God. Joseph had a dream, a vision, but his brothers hated him because of it. Real dreams from God provoke hatred and anger. The seething anger of Satan rekindles when he sees a man who has discovered God's vision for his life and begins to pursue it. Satan is even angrier when he sees a church that understands its vision and purpose. A church that has forsaken everything to pursue its God-given vision becomes a real threat to the kingdom of darkness.

It is through vision that the manifold purposes of God on the earth are manifested and fulfilled. Therefore, before you begin to serve in the church, take time to understand the vision of the church and the unique divine pattern God has given to accomplish it. This will prevent confusion that often arises when one is serving.

Before founding Christ's Voice of Restoration Ministries, Prophet Tom Tirivangani received a vision from God. The vision he received had a profound impact on his life and outlook. It transformed his relationship with God and defined his calling.

Many leaders in the church cause trouble and confusion because they do not know the vision that Prophet Tom received from God. They do not understand the history of the church. Every man who is called by God is a man of vision and purpose. God will not use you until He has taught you and until you have come to understand His purpose for your life.

It took Abraham twenty years to connect with his mission. Moses spent forty years in the wilderness, and out of the depths of loneliness and desperation, a vision was born in him. God saw an opportunity one afternoon while Moses was tending the flock of Jethro, his father-in-law. It was in that moment that God called to him from the burning bush. Vision is often born at a moment of deep curiosity. Moses wanted to understand why the bush was in flames but not being consumed.

In the same way, God spoke to Prophet Tom Tirivangani in a moment of personal desperation. Two of his close friends had died in a road accident. The world around him seemed dark and hopeless. In that moment, he began to seek the Jesus Christ he had first heard about from his grandfather during the winter of 1974 in Zimbabwe.

It was on an early, cold June morning in 1974 that he first remembered hearing the name of Jesus Christ. But who was He? Where was He? How could He help him? These questions stayed with him for years. It was only much later that they began to make sense and carry meaning.

In this part of the book, I explain the vision that Prophet Tom received from God when he was commissioned to start the church. I take time to describe what happened before I received this profound vision and revelation.

The word of God says, "In the mouth of two or three witnesses shall every word be established" (2 Cor. 13.1). How did Prophet Tom know that God was calling him? Was it his revelation alone, or did he have witnesses who testified of his calling?

Beginning in the cold morning of June 1974, God began to show up in many ways in Prophet Tom's life. Somewhere near the end of that year, his grandmother Wanagwa died. Prophet Tom was very close to her. In that moment of despair and pain, something remarkable happened. The people in the village were stuck. His father was working in the city, and messages had to be sent to inform him of his mother's passing. People were gathering, but there was no money to feed the mourners. Miraculously, young Tom picked up a £10 note and ran to give it to his mother. How someone in that remote village could have dropped such an amount was astonishing. Little did Prophet Tom know at the time that it was God who had shown up.

From that time onward, his life became a journey marked by miracles, signs, and wonders.

Another remarkable incident happened around March 1976. Tom's mother was almost killed by Zimbabwean freedom fighters. They summoned her to follow them, and under the compulsion of fear, she attempted to go. But she chose the path they were taking, and her youngest son, Bernard, strapped on her back, began to cry. When she turned in the direction of safety, the baby calmed down. Encouraged by her daughter Gertrude, she fled to safety. That very night, the concentrated refugee camps where they had been staying were attacked. The family had to walk about 35 kilometers on foot. When they arrived at East Hunyani, the Mudzi River was flooded. A miracle occurred. One man, standing alone at the river, helped each of the twenty members of the group cross safely to the other side.

The question remains: How did six families live in a three-bedroom house between 1977 and 1980? It is still a mystery today. But it proves a simple truth: there is always room in a heart full of love.

Prophet Tom often refers to his father as "God's General." He was a tall and towering figure, a man of great compassion and love, a man of unparalleled generosity. He loved quietness and despised strife.

Prophet Tom's father, Kumanda Clement, was his greatest mentor. His way of life left a lasting impact on his son.

We fast-forward to the time when I was a practicing lawyer in Harare. Many pastors would come to me and say they wanted to start a church with me. It was puzzling. Why would a pastor want to start a church with a drunkard, an alcoholic lawyer? It made no sense at the time, but now the picture is much clearer.

When I had surrendered my life to Christ and was living in the United Kingdom, many people began to prophesy that I was called by God. I vividly remember a woman named Gretta Chikwawawa. Her husband, Jonathan, called me from Leeds when I was in Coventry. He told me that God had sent me to pray for them. I responded, "How could this be? You are elders in the church, and I am just a deacon. How can you come to me?" But as God would have it, He answered my prayer for them. Today, Gretta and Jonathan Chikwawawa are bishops in Forward in Faith Ministries.

When I met Apostle Ezekiel Guti in the city of Birmingham in 2002, he told me that God had called me and wanted to use me. For many years, God used me in Forward in Faith International Church. In 2003, after a church conference in Birmingham, a man of God named Mediline Phiri from Zambia stayed with us for a month. Before he returned home, he called my wife and me and shared a prophetic word. He told me that God had called me and that I had to shut down my business and surrender my career.

Although I resisted at first, I eventually surrendered after experiencing a series of tragic events. I lost the entire fortune I had worked for over many years. It was through this loss and divine encounter that I finally gave in to the call of God on my life.

Now, as I explain the vision that God gave me, I urge you to read with understanding and humility. This vision is what guides my life, how I lead in the Church of God, and how I relate with people and the church. It is a vision I have sworn to uphold and implement.

I am willing to lose friends to defend the vision that God has entrusted to me. Through this vision, many souls will be saved, many churches will be planted, many ministers of God will be released into their callings, and many nations will be brought back to God. Those who uphold this vision will receive a remarkable blessing and inheritance from the God who has called and commissioned me.

A Remarkable Baptism

Before I begin sharing the actual vision I received from the Lord, there is one thing I feel compelled to speak about: my baptism. It was a unique experience and an important part of my spiritual journey, one that I must share.

I was born into a Catholic family and, as is the tradition, I was baptized as a young boy. I have no personal recollection of that event; I only know of it through the stories my mother and father told me. But when I was born again, I chose to be baptized a second time, though to me, it was truly my first.

This reminds me of the account found in the book of Acts 19. 1–6. It reads:

> "And it happened, while Apollos was at Corinth, that Paul, having passed through the upper regions, came to Ephesus. And finding some disciples he said to them, 'Did you receive the Holy Spirit when you believed?'
>
> So they said to him, 'We have not so much as heard whether there is a Holy Spirit.'
>
> And he said to them, 'Into what then were you baptized?'
>
> So they said, 'Into John's baptism.'

Then Paul said, 'John indeed baptized with a baptism of repentance, saying to the people that they should believe on Him who would come after him, that is, on Christ Jesus.'

When they heard this, they were baptized in the name of the Lord Jesus. And when Paul had laid hands on them, the Holy Spirit came upon them, and they spoke with tongues and prophesied. Now the men were about twelve in all."

This is an incredible story of gigantic spiritual significance. When I believe in the lord Jesus, I too baptized again in the name of the Lord Jesus. It took place at the Full Gospel New Testament Church of God in Coventry, United Kingdom, and I was baptized by Pastor Leonard McDonald. That night, my life was transformed. My hunger for God deepened, and a fire was kindled in my soul. I remember that my wife, Colline, was also baptized that night. The church was full of faithful believers who had come to witness this August occasion.

What followed that baptism, many months later, was truly remarkable.

I had a vision from the Lord. In the vision, I was taken to the nation of Israel, and I found myself standing in the middle of the Jordan River, being baptized by the Lord Jesus Himself . As I stood in the water, I saw many doves descending on the river. There were a number of us being baptized, and I watched many people running and chasing to catch their doves. What was remarkable was that my dove came form heaven and descended gently upon my head.

From that day, my life changed and was never the same. My zeal for God increased day by day. My desire to pray and seek the word burned within me. I have sought the Lord in many ways, and although I have gone through many discouraging times, I have never been discouraged in spirit. I do not carry bitterness, only holy anger when I see people straying away from the Lord.

Over time, I have com to understand what it means to be one with the Lord and what it means to be taught by the Holy Spirit. There are spiritual things that I just know, my knowing is supernatural and beyond human comprehension.

I thank God for this vision, and as you read the vision, you ought to understand what kind of a man has been entrusted with this vision. Take care and caution as you read the revelation I received from the Lord.

The Revelation from God to His Servant Prophet Tom Tirivangani

Every true vision has the word of God as its anchor and source. A true vision must be birthed in the Spirit and must find its support in the word of God. I begin by turning to the word of God:

> "But I make known to you, brethren, that the gospel which was preached by me is not according to man. For I neither received it from man, nor was I taught it, but it came through the revelation of Jesus Christ" (Gal. 1.11–12).

This vision I am about to share with you did come from a man, nor was it taught to me. It is a vision that came directly from God. It must be understood as the word from God and from our Lord Jesus Christ, who is the chief Shepherd and the cornerstone of this vision. As you read the vision, I urge you to do so prayerfully and reverentially, knowing that you are connecting with the purpose and vision of our God, not only for our generation, but for those to come.

One night, I had an incredible dream and a visitation from the Lord. He showed me a group of shepherds who were herding cattle, but they left their post and began playing soccer. The cattle strayed and started destroying the cornfield of someone. Then the voice of God called out and said, "Go and take the ball and direct them to go back to herding and tending the cattle." After I completed the task, a new revelation came from heaven.

Behold, before me stood a well-prepared field, ready for sowing or planting seed. A sower stood in the middle of the field planting seed. The Lord asked, "What is he doing?" I replied, "He is sowing seed." The Lord said, "What kind of seed?" I answered, "Groundnuts." The Lord said, "Look closely. What kind?" The vision zoomed in. I looked again and saw that the groundnuts were roasted. The Lord asked, "Can such a seed germinate?" I answered, "No." Then the Lord spoke clearly:

> "'Go and stand in my house and proclaim this message. The shepherds I have sent have led my people astray. From the least to the greatest, all are greedy for gain. Prophets and priests alike practice deceit. They dress the wounds of my people as though they were not serious.
>
> I command you and send you as a prophet unto the nations to go and call my people back to me,' says the Lord. 'Go and tell them to return to me, because the days are coming,' declares the Lord, 'when my voice shall be heard by nations as I announce the time of the restoration of my people, and now is the time.
>
> I shall gather the outcasts, the lame, the rejected, and the despised and make them into a strong nation. My house shall be called a House of Restoration. I am He, Jesus Christ, whom they crucified, but see, now I am risen and live forevermore. I am He who shall restore the outcasts, the lame, and the lowly into a strong nation.

The nations shall know that I am the Alpha and the Omega, and I am the Restorer. I will use you mightily to raise the standard of my righteousness and holiness before kings and governors of the nations, and you shall be called a preacher of righteousness.

I will use you to root out and pull down, to build up and to plant. Many mighty signs and wonders I will perform through you, and the fear of God will return to the nations. Many people will come from faraway lands to see the light and many nations will gather among you. Therefore, prepare yourself and arise and speak everything I have commanded you.

Do not be afraid of their faces, for I am with you. I have made you a fortified pillar for my name's sake. Be bold and courageous. They will fight against you, but they shall never prevail against you, for I am with you,' says the Lord, 'to deliver you.'"

4

Understanding the Vision of the Church

Understanding the vision of the church is very important if you are going to fulfil your purpose and place in the church. It is also important if you are going to function effectively in order to fulfill the vision.

Take note of this. According to Proverbs 29.18, "Where there is no vision, the people perish…" (KJV). The vision of the church gives life and purpose to those who serve under it. The vision of the church brings direction and focus to the church. Without it, we become like a plane without a pilot and a destination or direction. The vision is like the compass in a plane that gives direction to the pilot. Even in the midst of the storms, where visibility is sometimes obscured, the pilot and his crew rely heavily and solely on the compass for direction.

The prophet of God has been given a compass by God for direction for the church. That compass is the vision. Every true church of God is a unique institution with a clear mandate or vision. Although all churches are part of the body of Christ, each church must have a unique purpose for its existence.

It must be understood and not overemphasized that the church is a people called out by God with one clear agenda and vision. Members of the church must not bring their own agendas to the church. Multiple agendas, no matter how noble or good, will bring conflict and strife into the church. The spirit of offense operates in a church where the leaders push their own personal agendas. If things do not go the way they desire in the church, they become offended. In a church with multiple agendas, people tend to form cliques, groups, or camps.

This was exactly the problem in the Corinthian church. Remember, some were saying, "We are of Paul," and others, "We are of Apollos." In other words, some sections of the church preferred Paul as their leader, while others preferred Apollos. This effectively brought division in the church and displaced Christ from His rightful position as the head of the church. Christ is the Bridegroom of the Bride. He is the Owner of the church. This must be understood by every leader and every member of the church. The vision is Christ's vision for the church, and He has entrusted the stewardship of that vision to one man.

God entrusted Moses with the vision of bringing the people of Israel out of bondage in Egypt. God gave Noah the vision to build the ark.

In the same way, God has given Prophet Tom Tirivangani the vision to call His people back to the Lord and to the true gospel of our Lord Jesus Christ. Therefore, every member of the church is called to follow and uphold this vision.

Without following one vision, people tend to focus on their own personal agendas rather than on how they can serve God through the vision He has given to the man of God. Conflict and suspicion will dominate the atmosphere instead of unity, as everyone pursues their own ambitions (1 Cor.1.10–17). We do not want to see this worldly behaviour taking root in the house of the living God.

I urge you, as Paul did with the believers and leaders at the Corinthian church, "Aim for perfection, listen to my appeal, be of one mind" (2 Cor.13.11). When we focus on the vision, we allow the potential and gifts of every person in the church to be recognized and utilized for the glory of God.

To achieve this, everyone must understand the vision of the church and follow it. According to Habakkuk 2.2–3, we are instructed to:

"Write the vision and make it plain on tablets, that he may run who reads it. For the vision is yet for an appointed time; but at the end it will speak, and it will not lie. Though it tarries, wait for it; because it will surely come, it will not tarry."

5

Essential Aspects of the Vision

I have decided to break down the vision to make it plain for you:

1. **"The shepherds I've sent have led my people astray."**

Some churches of God have lost its way. Many pastors in our generation have, in various ways, misled the flock. Outwardly, the church may appear righteous, but inwardly it is often corrupted and polluted. Therefore, we must examine carefully the practices we observe in other churches to ensure they are scripturally sound before embracing them. Like the Berean believers (Acts 17:11), we must test all things against the Scriptures. Sound doctrine and a thorough understanding of the Word of God are foundational in our ministry. This is why we hold weekly Bible Study sessions and maintain a Bible College at the church. The Bible, not textbooks or other Christian literature, must remain our primary source for teaching and learning.

2. **"They are greedy and preach for gain."**

The love of money and the pursuit of personal gain have seduced many pastors in this generation. Many preach not to advance the Kingdom of God but to build personal empires rooted in materialism, distorting the teachings of our Lord Jesus Christ. We will never preach for money, nor will we make money the focus of our message. However, this does not mean we are against giving. We strongly believe in tithes, offerings, and giving for the purpose of building God's church. However, the aim must always be to advance the Gospel of the Kingdom and not to promote materialism.

3. "I command you to go and call My people to return to me."

Fulfilling the great commission (Mark 16.15) is very important for us as a ministry. We are called to go into the highways and byways to witness and win souls. We cannot wait for the people to come to us. We must go and call them back to the Lord. This is why we engage in street evangelism and outreach, and every leader is expected to support and participate in this mission.

4. "I am raising the lame, rejected, and despised into a strong nation."

We must see drug addicts, prostitutes, alcoholics, and the marginalized as potential fellow soldiers in this mission. We cannot shun or look down upon the poor and the rejected. In our ministry, these are the very people God desires to use mightily for His glory and to turn them into strong nations.

5. "I want to restore my people, and now is the time."

We believe in the restoration of broken marriages, deliverance from demonic oppression, and divine healing. Signs and wonders will be the norm in this ministry. We must be a prayerful, faith-filled, united, and loving church. Faith works through love. As leaders, we cannot walk in the spirit of competition, self-promotion, or selfishness. These attitudes will hinder the move of God. We must serve in humility and love.

6. "I have made you a Prophet unto the nations, and many nations will be among you."

The prophetic and apostolic mandate I received from God is a calling to be His messenger to the nations. God has used me to speak prophetically to individuals, churches, and entire nations with accuracy and power. As part of this mandate, our church is composed of people from different nationalities and backgrounds. Our church is not a one nation, one nationality or one race church. We reject all racial and nationalistic labels. We are not a "white church" because we are based in Canada, nor are we a "black" or "African church" because the man of God is black. We are the Church of God. Our apostolic mandate includes the planting of churches in every nation of the world.

7. "Many people will come from afar to see the light."

This church will be filled with people from every nation. Every leader must be ready to welcome and accommodate individuals from different cultures and backgrounds. Prejudice and condescending attitudes have no place in this house. We are committed to walking in love, unity, fellowship, and mutual respect as we serve God together. By His grace, this is what we will continually strive to do.

6

Our Mission

1. To Boldly preach and proclaim the true Gospel of the Kingdom of God in season and out of season, and wait to see the harvest of millions of souls coming to Christ. This will be accomplished through the planting of churches in every city, every nation, and to the ends of the earth.
2. To be instruments in the hands of God as He establishes a church modeled after the first church in the book of Acts (being in one accord, prayerful, fellowshipping through the breaking of bread, healing of the sick, feeding and clothing the hungry and poor, and faithful preaching of the Gospel.
3. To pray fervently for the revival across the world and for the fire of God to fall afresh upon His people.
4. To be a church that hears and does the Word of God. We are called to live out the Word of God to the fullest and to be a church that bears the fruit of the Holy Spirit. Christ said, "You will know them by their fruits. Do men gather grapes from thornbushes or figs from thistles? Even so, every good tree bears good fruit, but a bad tree bears bad fruit. A good tree cannot bear bad fruit, nor can a bad tree bear good fruit. Every tree that does not bear good fruit is cut down and thrown into the fire. Therefore by their fruits you will know them" (Matt. 7.16–20).

7

The Pattern for the Church

"Make yourself an ark of gopherwood; make rooms in the ark, and cover it inside and outside with pitch. And this is how you shall make it: The length of the ark shall be three hundred cubits, its width fifty cubits, and its height thirty cubits. You shall make a window for the ark, and you shall finish it to a cubit from above; and set the door of the ark in its side. You shall make it with lower, second, and third decks" (Gen. 6.14–16).

In Genesis 6, God instructed Noah to make an ark and proceeded to provide a detailed design or pattern for Noah to follow.

It is important to understand that God does not just give a vision. God also gives a pattern on how the vision will be implemented. It is fundamental that Leaders have a deep understanding of the vision and the pattern of the church. These two aspects are critical in obeying the will of God. Please pay careful attention as you read the pattern

1. A divine plan produces divine results. Man-made plans cannot produce divine results. When God calls a man, He always provides the pattern. He called Noah and provided him a pattern on how to build the ark. On October 21, 2008, God revealed His plan and pattern to His servant. This is the pattern the church leaders must be careful to follow. God also revealed to His servant that the church will move from North America and go to Europe via Eastern Europe. The church will enter Europe through Poland, the Czech Republic, and the surrounding regions. The church will establish orphanages in many places around the world.
2. It is not I as the prophet, or you as the believer, deacon, or elder, who builds the church. God alone is the one who adds to the church. Psalm 127.1–2 says, "Unless the Lord builds the house, they labour in vain who build it; unless the Lord guards the city, the watchman stays awake in vain."
3. We must lift the name of Jesus Christ in the church. If we lift up the name of the Lord Jesus Christ in the city, in the nation, and to the people, God Himself will draw all men unto Himself. We must share the gospel, especially with people who are not born again or have backslidden. We pray for Jesus to become their personal Lord and Saviour. The backslidden are to be assisted in rededicating their lives to Christ. We as a church must then disciple them, bring them into the house of God, and equip them for the work of the ministry, as written in Eph-

esians 4.11–12: "And He Himself gave some to be apostles, some prophets, some evangelists, and some pastors and teachers, for the equipping of the saints for the work of ministry, for the edifying of the body of Christ."

4. Soul-winning is a very important aspect of our assignment as a church. We must not just sit in our offices or homes and enjoy our salvation, but instead we must go to the byways, shopping malls, and into our neighbourhoods and spread the gospel. If you do not win souls for Christ, it is clear that you are practicing foolishness. The Word of God testifies that he who wins souls is wise. In keeping with this mandate, every member of our church must engage in command evangelism.

5. We must be willing to receive people who are hurt or unhappy in their churches and are trying to find a new church in the spirit of love and fellowship. We must not help or encourage them to criticize the leaders or pastors of where they are coming from. Instead, we must pray for them and encourage them to forgive the people who hurt them. Always remember that there are two sides to every story. The Bible says do not receive an accusation against an elder except at the testimony of two or three witnesses. The most important thing is to remind the brother or sister that there is healing power in forgiveness, irrespective of what happened to them. Remind them that Jesus is the answer, and our eyes must be on Him and Him alone.

6. The youth is the key to future generations. Any generation that fails to take care of its youth is heading for disaster. In the past, the church has failed to properly transmit the gospel to the youth, and many churches are closing down as the older generation is taken into retirement homes. Now is the time to take the gospel to the youth and children and prepare them as the future church.

7. We must show love and respect to all people of God and honour other servants of God. There are many servants of God out

there doing the work of God. There are many other living churches around the world. We are called to honour the churches of God that are authentic and doing their best to reach out to lost souls.

8. Our church is a fellowshipping church, and we encourage house-to-house fellowship to enable us to minister to one another and to our neighbours. It is important that we spend time together and grow into a large family of God.
9. When we witness about Christ, our witnessing must not be about comparing our ministry to other ministries. It must be about Christ working through our ministry. We must avoid elevating ourselves above others, although we cannot avoid testifying about the works of God in our local fellowship or church.
10. We must not compete with any church. We must strive to demonstrate the fruit of the Holy Spirit in our church through the lives of the members (Gal 5.22–23). We must not have a critical spirit, but must learn to compliment.
11. Our lives must reflect the character of Christ. Therefore, we must emphasize to the believers the importance of showing the fruit of the Holy Spirit.
12. We must never stop loving people, no matter how many times they wrong us. We must keep on loving them while correcting them and praying for them.
13. We must live the Word, have faith, and repent continually. We must keep on renewing our commitment to Christ daily.
14. We must not get to a point where we feel we know it all. We must keep learning, listening, and praying. The four pillars of the church are prayer, prayer, prayer, and prayer. Prayer is work, but prayer works (Luke 18.1).
15. Every leader is expected to invest time in personal spiritual growth in order to serve God. It is the responsibility of the leader to be available for mentorship (equipping) in order to serve God to the best of their ability.

16. The leaders are expected to serve with the spirit of excellence, ensuring that they are punctual for meetings or church service, keep proper records of their work, are accountable in all areas of their personal life, and are fully devoted and committed to the work of God.
17. Leaders must ensure they maintain proper respect and confidentiality regarding the information they receive in the course of their ministry. They make an undertaking to ensure that information received during the course of ministry will not be abused.
18. The believers and the leaders must commit themselves to giving tithes and offerings as a way of honoring God. No one shall be a leader unless he tithes and gives offerings faithfully.
19. Members of the church are expected to attend church and prayer meetings regularly and faithfully.
20. Members of the church are expected to find a place or ministry in the church where they use their gifts for the glory of God.

8

Whose Church is it?

The church belongs to our Lord Jesus Christ: "I will build My church, and the gates of Hades shall not prevail against it" (Matt.16:18). The Church is Jesus' idea and is founded upon Him, Jesus Christ, the Rock of Ages. Every man of God must be commissioned by our Lord and Saviour Jesus Christ.

Jeremiah was called and commissioned when he was a youth:

Then the word of the Lord came to me, saying: "Before I formed you in the womb I knew you; before you were born I sanctified you; I ordained you a prophet to the nations." Then said I: "Ah, Lord God! Behold, I cannot speak, for I am a youth." But the Lord said to me: "Do not say, 'I am a youth,' for you shall go to all to whom I send you, and whatever I command you, you shall speak. Do not be afraid of their faces, for I am with you to deliver you," says the Lord. Then the Lord put forth His hand and touched my mouth, and the Lord said to me: "Behold, I have put My words in your mouth. See, I have this day set you over the nations and over the kingdoms, to root out and to pull down, to destroy and to throw down, to build and to plant" (Jer. 1.4–10).

The word of the Lord literally came to Jeremiah, and he did not speak from his own imagination as the false prophets did, like Hananiah:

And it happened in the same year, at the beginning of the reign of Zedekiah king of Judah, in the fourth year and in the fifth month, that

Hananiah the son of Azur, the prophet who was from Gibeon, spoke to me in the house of the Lord in the presence of the priests and of all the people, saying, "Thus speaks the Lord of hosts, the God of Israel…" (Jer. 28.1–2).

Jeremiah spoke as God revealed His word and His will to him. Paul was converted on his way to Damascus and was called to preach the Gospel of our Lord Jesus Christ:

And he said, "Who are You, Lord?" Then the Lord said, "I am Jesus, whom you are persecuting. It is hard for you to kick against the goads." So he, trembling and astonished, said, "Lord, what do You want me to do?" Then the Lord said to him, "Arise and go into the city, and you will be told what you must do" (Acts 9.5–6).

In the same way, the Lord has appeared to Prophet Tom in visions and dreams on several occasions. The word of the Lord came to him, saying:

"The shepherds I have sent have led My people astray. They became greedy, and they preach for gain. They have made My house a house of merchandise. In their quest for profit, they sowed roasted seed and proclaimed that it was My word. I am against them unless they repent.

As for you, I knew you before you were born. I have called you as a prophet to the nations, and I want you to restore them.

My house shall be called a House of Restoration. Fear not, for I am with you. See now, I am gathering the lame, the lost, the despised, and the rejected into a strong nation."

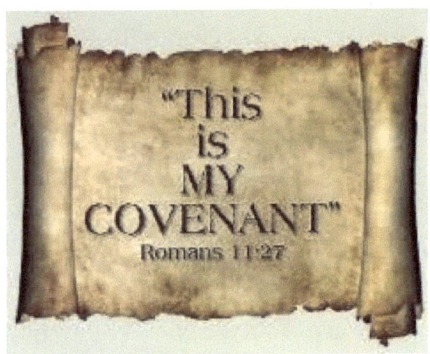

On that day, God gave me His covenant and sealed my calling and vocation: that I am called as a prophet unto the nations. The church is not my idea; it is a clear commission from our Lord Jesus Christ. I therefore do not speak on own account. I lift up Him who sent me, our Lord Jesus Christ of Nazareth. Those who receive me as a Prophet shall receive a Prophet's reward. These are the few things we want you to take note of as you join the ministry and become a member of this body, Christ's Voice Restoration Ministries.

1. We are a soul-winning church (Luke 9.10). Jesus did not come to please the religious crowd. He did not come to pander to the social elite. Jesus entered the world to save sinners. When we look back at the three-year ministry of our Lord Jesus Christ, we see an example of what we must do. Jesus reached out to men and women, the young and the old, the poor and the rich, the powerful and the forgotten, the demon-possessed and the politically connected. He came to save sinners of all shapes, sizes, statuses, nationalities, ethnicities, tribes, and races. He came to save you and me.
2. For us, as it was for our Lord Jesus, the salvation of souls is the greatest miracle that can ever happen in a person's life. The best thing that will ever happen to anyone is not winning a million-dollar lottery; it is being born again. That is when you experience a new birth, and your soul is regenerated. Paul de-

clares, "Therefore, if anyone is in Christ, he is a new creation; old things have passed away; behold, all things have become new" (2 Cor.5.17). We preach repentance as both the key to restoration and the door to healing. "Repent, for the kingdom of heaven is at hand" (Matt.3.2). "Repent therefore and be converted, that your sins may be blotted out, so that times of refreshing may come from the presence of the Lord" (Acts 3.19). See also 2 Chronicles 7.14.

3. We are a prayerful church, both at a personal and a corporate level. Members of the church are charged to commit themselves to a life of prayer and devotion to God. Jesus did not hang out with the wild bunch in order to become like them; He was among them to call them to repentance. Likewise, we are called to live in holiness while interceding for the lost.

4. We are a church that believes the Holy Bible is the Word of the Living God. It is the supernaturally inspired Word of God, written by the Holy Spirit. It is the only true ground of Christian unity and fellowship. We believe the Holy Bible is the eternal tribunal by whose standards all men and nations will be judged.

9

A Word on Being One Body

The church is a gift given by God to mankind. It has its place in the Kingdom of God. Just as it has its rightful place, the church has also been ordained by God to function in a specific way. The Church of God has been designed by God to work as a team. In order to succeed in its mandate and vision, the church must work together as one body with different gifts (1 Cor.12.12-27).

Jesus showed us the standard and the method to follow for effective, fruitful, and productive leadership for the glory of God. Each leader must find his or her place in the church. After discovering your place, you must commit yourself to being part of the body or team and dedicate yourself to the success of that body. Every leader must understand that success in ministry or calling is only possible when individual gifts are placed into the team basket. No man is an island; no one can succeed alone. You need others. You need the body, and the body needs you. You are important to the body, and the body is important to you.

Jesus had a team of twelve disciples, each man assigned a specific task and mandate. This is how He carried out His ministry. If we are His disciples, we need to follow this pattern in order to impact the world. With only twelve men committed to the cause of the Kingdom of God, the church has risen to become the most powerful and effective institution in the world today.

Our church has been called to function as a team. Never think you can do it all by yourself. Leaders must be constantly searching to see who can be part of their ministry or team. Do not be overprotective of the vision to the point of killing it by refusing to allow others to contribute. Not everyone who joins the team will be perfect. Some may have flaws. Some may even betray the team. But remember, love never fails.

Do your part. Train your team to understand the vision and to remain faithful to the cause of the Kingdom of God. Ultimately, we must trust in the Lord with all our hearts and lean not on our own understanding. As we acknowledge God in all our ways, He will direct our paths to His glory (Prov. 3.5–6).

Below are the core teams the church needs in order to drive the vision forward:

1. **The Vision Team:** This team ensures that every newcomer understands and commits to the vision. It also ensures that long-standing members remain committed and connected to the vision.
2. **Administration Team:** This team is responsible for the day-to-day administration of the church. They ensure that everything in the church is done in order and in decency. They make sure that all records are kept accurately and properly to maintain the integrity of the church of God.
3. **Evangelism Team:** Winning souls is the greatest mission and mandate of the church. The team ensures that the church grows numerically by bringing new souls into the Kingdom of God.
4. **Hospitality & Welfare Team:** People who come to church may forget the sermon, but they will not forget love. This team often referred to as the "Love Team," ensures love remains alive

and active among the members of the church. No one should feel left out or neglected.

5. **The Finance Team:** This team ensures that the church is financially sound and well provided for, and that no bills remain unpaid. We must not bring the name of God into disrepute by failing to honor financial obligations.
6. **Teaching Ministry:** This team is responsible for making disciples of all nations, especially the new converts who are coming to church (Matt.28.19–20). They ensure that every believer receives sound doctrine and grows into a disciple of Christ.
7. **Praise and Worship Team:** This team leads the church in learning and practicing to praise and worship God through music; helping the church to glorify God in spirit and in truth.
8. **Youth Ministry Team:** We cannot neglect our youth. They are the future church. This team ensures that the youth are connected to the life of the church, worship, and service to God in preparation to carry the church into the future.
9. **Men and Women's Ministries:** Though they function as two distinct ministries, each ensures that men and women find their place in both the church and the Kingdom of God. These ministries help their members remain active in the church and contribute to transforming nations for God's glory.
10. **The Prophetic Ministry:** This team is responsible for teaching about and maintaining the prophetic ministry. It ensures that the people of God benefit from the prophetic grace given to the man of God and the church.

10

A Word on Church Membership

The issue of church membership is an important element of any truly living church. A genuine and true church must take church membership is a important and an indispensable and vital feature of a vibrant church. Christ voice of restoration is called to be a model church in the 21st century, where church commitment is a very rare commodity ,it is sad that the 21st century church is fluid and unstable in so far as church membership is concerned, it is very common for Christians to come from one church to another. In most cases maybe a member of your church has been a "member" of almost every church in the city. This was rare of churches in the 19th century going back to the first century. In this context it is important to address the question of church membership to ensure that Christ's voice of restoration ministries is a stable, vibrant and living church taking the true gospel to the nations.

The biggest issue with unstable church members is that they are not willing to submit to the church authorities and be accountable to a body of believers. Although we are members of the body of Christ and of the universal church generally, but God has called us to bring to belong to a local body or a local assembly of members of the body of Christ.

When a believer neglects or refuse to belong to a local body of believers they fail to recognise the authority of the scripture and this may result in them missing the blessing and the opportunities associated in belongings to a local body of believers. In this part of the vision book we will deal with the issue of church membership because it is important that every genuine born again believer understand what church membership is and why God has commissioned it for the local assembly.

The Definition of church membership

When someone gives their life to Christ and is born again, as described in 2 Corinthians 5.17: "Therefore, if anyone is in Christ, he is a new creation; old things have passed away; behold, all things have become new," they automatically become a member of the body of Christ. "For by one Spirit we were all baptized into one body—whether Jews or Greeks, whether slaves or free—and have all been made to drink into one Spirit" (1 Cor. 12.13).

When a believer is born again, they are united with Christ and, in turn, are also united with other born-again believers who make up the body of Christ.

In order for a believer to qualify as a member of a local assembly, such as Christ's Voice of Restoration, they must commit themselves alongside other believers to God's ordained, divine, and specific purpose for that local assembly. This purpose includes receiving instruction from God's Word and advancing the vision of the assembly.

> "Till I come, give attention to reading, to exhortation, to doctrine" (1 Tim. 4.13).

> "Preach the word! Be ready in season and out of season. Convince, rebuke, exhort, with all longsuffering and teaching" (2 Tim. 4.2).

The believer must also commit to serving and edifying others through the proper use and exercise of their spiritual gifts (Rom.12.3–8; 1 Cor.12.4–31; 1 Pet. 4.10–11).

Participation in church ordinances is also essential. Jesus commanded, "Do this in remembrance of Me" (Luke 22.19), and the early believers "continued steadfastly in the apostles' doctrine and fellowship, in the breaking of bread, and in prayers" (Acts 2.42). Believers must also accept their responsibility to proclaim the true gospel to the lost, as commissioned by Christ in Matthew 28.18–20.

The believer must also submit to the spiritual care and authority of pastors, elders, or deacons whom God has ordained and planted in any local assembly of Christ's Voice of Restoration.

Although many teachers and scholars argue that formal church membership is not a requirement, we in Christ's Voice of Restoration Ministries believe that there is ample evidence of church membership within the New Testament. We therefore believe that every believer is called to belong to a local assembly. Most of the letters or epistles in the New Testament were written to members of local churches, which demonstrates the reality of committed membership.

It is also important to examine the New Testament scriptures to recognize and understand the sanctity of the membership in home or house churches. Consider the following examples:

> "The churches of Asia greet you. Aquila and Priscilla greet you heartily in the Lord, with the church that is in their house" (1 Cor. 16.19).

> "Greet the brethren who are in Laodicea, and Nymphas and the church that is in his house" (Col. 4.15).

> "Greet Philologus and Julia, Nereus and his sister, and Olympas, and all the saints who are with them" (Rom. 16.15).

> "To the beloved Apphia, Archippus our fellow soldier, and to the church in your house" (Phil. 1.2).

In the early church, coming to Christ as a new convert meant coming to the church of Jesus Christ. It is clear that the idea in the 21st century "believers" of experiencing salvation without belonging to a local assembly is not found in the New Testament churches. When believers repented and were baptized, they were added to the local assembly.

> Acts 2:41 says, "Then those who gladly received his word were baptized; and that day about three thousand souls were added to them."
>
> Acts 5:14 affirms, "And believers were increasingly added to the Lord, multitudes of both men and women."
>
> Acts 16:5 also testifies, "So the churches were strengthened in the faith, and increased in number daily."

The believers were summoned to belong to a local assembly where they devoted themselves to the apostles' teaching, to fellowship, and to the breaking of bread with fellow believers.

This is the pattern Christ's Voice of Restoration is called by God to follow. Therefore, every believer must be added to a list or a register of members belonging to the local assembly as modeled in 1 Timothy 5. 9-10:

"Do not let a widow under sixty years old be taken into the number, and not unless she has been the wife of one man, well reported for good works: if she has brought up children, if she has lodged strangers, if she has washed the saints' feet, if she has relieved the afflicted, if she has diligently followed every good work."

11

Leadership Structure

The first level of leadership is known as the Council of the Twelve.

This council functions as the general leadership body of the church. It consists of workers, deacons, elders, pastors, and bishops who have been recognized for their faithfulness and commitment to ministry (Mark 3.16–19). These individuals are recommended by their local church leaders and are then commissioned and confirmed by the second level of leadership.

The second level of leadership is called the Apostolic and Prophetic Council.

This council is composed of esteemed servants of God, pillars in the church, who have proven themselves in spiritual service and, in some cases, in governmental leadership as well. As Paul wrote, "and when James, Cephas, and John, who seemed to be pillars, perceived the grace that had been given to me, they gave me and Barnabas the right hand of fellowship" (Gal. 2.9).

These two leadership levels ensure that the church is governed in order, by the Spirit of God, and according to divine patterns established in scripture and revealed through prophetic insight.

12

The Blessing of Serving in Another Man's Ministry

Now It's Time for You to Be a Part of This Dream. You've taken the time to read the dream God gave to me. Now is the time for you to make up your mind and join wholeheartedly in the dream, the vision, the church that will radically impact the spiritual condition of our nation and our generation.

To partner with Jesus Christ in His mission to free humanity from the shackles of sin, poverty, and hopelessness is the greatest dream that can ever be known. Join the Church of the Living God as we prepare for the second coming of our Lord Jesus Christ, ensuring that no one is left behind as we march toward Heaven.

Heaven is our destination. Heaven is our dream place!

We are determined to obey God and do everything necessary to make it to Heaven. That is the greatest dream we have; that when the saints go marching in, you and I will be in that number. We want to take our rightful place in Heaven. We are citizens of Heaven. Today, we are mere pilgrims on the earth.

Do not worry about where you are right now in your faith. You can start from where you are. Do not be overwhelmed by what you see or what you've heard. Every small step counts.

Jesus Christ wants you to rise up and join Him in bringing the Good News to humanity.

Thank you for deciding to join the dream. Know that you will never regret the decision you have made to take ownership of this dream.

Congratulations, your walk-in service to God starts **NOW**.

www.ingramcontent.com/pod-product-compliance
Lightning Source LLC
Chambersburg PA
CBHW040258010526
44119CB00041B/488